Looking for a car? Let a pro show you the ropes!

Edward Roop knows what goes on behind the scenes at car dealerships—an automotive authority, lecturer, and consultant, he has over twenty years of experience in the automotive and retail industries. He knows what customers can do to avoid being taken. Now he shares his inside information in *Best Deals for New Wheels*—a unique guide for anyone who's thinking of buying or leasing a car.

Includes:

- **a handy test-drive checklist**

- **tips on getting the most for your trade-in**

- **information on services and warranties**

- **the truth about "special deals"**

- **and much more!**

Best DEALS FOR NEW WHEELS

HOW TO SAVE MONEY WHEN BUYING OR LEASING A CAR

EDWARD ROOP

B

BERKLEY BOOKS, NEW YORK

Previously published in a revised form by the author under the title *Everything You Will Need to Know When Buying or Leasing a Car.*

This Berkley book contains the revised text of the original edition. It has been completely reset in a typeface designed for easy reading, and was printed from new film.

BEST DEALS FOR NEW WHEELS

A Berkley Book / published by arrangement with the author

PRINTING HISTORY
R.I. LTD. edition published 1991
Berkley revised edition / October 1992

To Oz

Contents

Introduction

AFTER A HOME, A NEW CAR IS THE largest purchase most people will make, and they will likely do it several times. It would appear to be obvious that so large an expense as this would be a very serious concern.

However, what I've found to be the case is that although people will think of it as an *important* purchase, most do not take it seriously, inasmuch as they are not really well equipped with specific knowledge or helpful information when they set out to buy the car. They are not too sure how to negotiate or when, whether to trade or not, what options to buy or not to buy and why, what services or warranties to consider, how best to finance or where to finance, or even if they should be buying or leasing in the first place. In a much too real sense, they just "wing it"!

The very same people who would not consider themselves careless in all varieties of matters, financial or otherwise, can be very cavalier in their approach to buying a car. People who readily consult with a lawyer or accountant, hire a plumber, or even refer to a cookbook before attempting a recipe—people who *regularly* make a point of seeking out the requisite "expertise" rather than testing their own capabilities—somehow feel confident that they're quite able to just go out and buy a car. They possess little or no knowledge of the process— a purchase that can cost tens of thousands of dollars; they "wing it." And this, I can assure you, can be a *very* costly mistake.

Right off, buying a car is vastly different from the purchase of most consumer goods in that you "bargain" for a car. This is common for most purchases in some cultures, but it is not something that the majority of Americans are adept at, so you are immediately at a disadvantage. You are part of a negotiation with a professional salesman who does it *every* day. He knows what buttons to push and when; not only that, but he most likely knows more about the product, the financing, the competition—in short, he has the upper hand. Professional car salesmen can be quite resourceful at parting you and your money, but at the same time, very adroit in mitigating your concerns and getting you to believe they've helped you to get a "really good deal." Please remember, if ever there was a classic oxymoron it is "car salesmen *helping* the customer to get a deal." At best you'll be wading through a lot of nonsense and shameless hokum; at worst you'll be faced with unscrupulous and blatant dishonesty.

I have written this book with the intention of enabling the car buyer to understand the process, make the correct choices, and then pay the lowest possible price. Believe me, it will really pay off to be informed when you set out to buy the car, because it's very probable that you will be venturing into a "den of thieves."

At the same time, I am aware that most people are not inclined to devote much time to the car-buying process: maybe a week or maybe a day—for some just one evening at a dealer. But if you spend a small amount of time and read this book first, I promise you, you'll be thankful later.

I'm also aware that although there are a lot of car lovers, there are countless others who view the need for a car in more practical terms, and still others for whom the car is nothing more than a boring and intrusive necessity. It is something you have to take care of and something that breaks—well, after all, that is correct. I've talked to people who would spend much more time researching and then looking for a new set of golf clubs or shopping for the "right" dress than they would buying a car. I point this out because it's my intention to keep that sort of thing in mind as I attempt to be realistic about who it is that I'm writing for. The simple fact here is that the vast majority of car buyers do not know the way they should go about buying; they end up unnecessarily accepting bad deals—they get "taken."

It may surprise you that the "average buyer" includes everyone: professional person or laborer, soldier or secretary, student or retiree. No matter if you're young or old, high income or low, male, female, very smart or very average, buying a subcompact or luxury car, I do not think I can overstate this fact: no one is immune, because when it comes to making the largest profit that he possibly can, the car salesman does not discriminate. You are *all* fair game. This may hurt your ego, but believe me, it is true. So, the fact is that I am writing for a very wide and diverse audience. How should I do this? What is appropriate?

It is my belief that a long book, full of every aspect of the automobile industry that relates to the business of selling and buying cars, although informative to a few, would be extremely counterproductive to most. Who really would read it? No single book should pretend to make you an expert. It will never enable you to question specifics like a trial lawyer when you're negotiating; nor could it teach you to think about a car like an automotive engineer. What should be accomplished, and therefore what I've tried to do, is to cover the important things in a manner relatively simple to grasp. Not too technical or too complicated, the book, rather, will stay focused on the primary goals of developing your ability to knowledgeably decide what you want and need, and then to fully comprehend and understand the negotiation process—what to *look* for and what to *look out* for.

Remember, in any negotiation or process that requires bargaining, INFORMATION IS POWER AND CONTROL. When you know everything that's in this book, then that should be sufficient to enable you to negotiate to your best advantage, get the best deal, and save as much money as possible.

—A. E.

Getting Ready
to Buy a Car
Decisions, Decisions

Choosing a Car/
Basic Considerations

T HE FIRST THING YOU MUST DO IS TO honestly and realistically figure out what you can afford or want to pay for a car, and you should also think about the car from the standpoint of *total* expenses. Consider that the average new car cost will be in excess of $15,000, or approximately $400 per month for an average three-year loan with a down payment. To this amount must be added an average of $65 for insurance and $140 for gas, oil, and repairs. As you can see, you are now looking at over $600 per month in rounded figures for relatively standard transportation.

To calculate what you can afford, prepare a realistic budget based on your monthly earned and unearned income. Before determining a maximum amount you will be willing to pay, confront yourself by realistically answering the following questions.

1. Why do you need a car and what is its purpose? For example: is it to be used for basic transportation, for recreation, or a combination, and how many passengers must it carry?

2. Relative to this, what type of car or model makes sense? Examples: coupe, sedan, hatchback, station wagon, van, convertible, etc. Also, give some consideration to size: subcompact to full-size.

3. How do these factors affect your choice: fuel economy, performance, style, comfort, reputation of car, image?

4. How long will you keep it and in what condition? Will you sell the car or trade it? How important is resale value to you?

5. How do you see yourself or want others to see you in relation to your car?

6. How much time will you devote to: comparison shopping, researching the

possibilities, implementing the information in this book?

Before you spend the money, draw yourself an honest picture both of what you need and want. Take the time now to write down your answers to each of the above questions, and keep them handy while you continue reading.

Researching the Car/ Specific Considerations

It's IMPORTANT THAT YOU KNOW AS much as you can about the particular car (or class of car) you would like to buy *prior* to talking to the salesman or working a deal. Being knowledgeable when you're ready to negotiate will eliminate one of the biggest advantages the salesman usually has. I've explained that "information is power," and if the salesman feels you can be influenced, fooled or misled, or simply flat-out lied to, then you are immediately at a serious disadvantage. I do not wish to imply that *all* salesmen are dishonest (some may just be less than well informed themselves), but common sense should suggest that *a buyer not rely on the very person who has to sell cars at the highest possible profit to make a living,* and furthermore, MUST provide the dealer with a high margin if he wishes to keep that job. As much as this may seem so obvious and logical, the simple fact is that the majority of car buyers get the bulk, if not all, of their information from the salesmen. What is truly unfortunate is that they know very little about the car industry and even less about the art of negotiation.

The following are different means by which you can get useful information that will go a long way toward making you knowledgeable about the car you want to buy.

- Get a new car price book that lists both the sticker price and the actual dealers' cost for the base car and all factory options; I recommend *Edmund's New Car Prices* (others, such as *Pace Buyer's Guide* and *Consumer's Guide,* are available). This book will allow you to know approximately what the dealer is making on each car, and, therefore, will be instrumental in your ability to negotiate the lowest amount he can accept. For similar reasons, educate yourself with regard to the prices of competing makes also.

- Obtain literature from dealers. These brochures will furnish you with information regarding available models, colors, and trim; standard equipment and options; warranties; dimensions; and technical specs such as horsepower, fuel consumption, EPA listing, etc. You can also send for this directly from the manufacturer. (See Appendix.)

· Various car magazines are available at the local bookseller, newsstand, and library. These can provide you with very specific information, technical and otherwise, along with test results and comparative data. But be aware, when reading opinions regarding a car, that although it may be an "expert" opinion, it can be as biased and subjective as any critic's opinion. Of the many car magazines that are published worldwide, few will agree on car of the year, best in class, best value, etc.

· Go to the bookstore or library and get the current consumer guides. The information here is usually objective.

· A very useful method of getting information regarding a specific model or make of car is through conversations with current owners. Should you have friends in the auto industry, they probably possess above average knowledge about cars; in the same vein, mechanics at private garages can provide you with interesting and informative insights.

- Attending a large auto show is an ideal way to preview all at one time many different makes and models that you're considering. If you have not yet made the basic decision about what you want to buy, you'll be able to look without having to fend off salesmen; at the same time, you can get all the pertinent literature, prices, etc.

Remember: Know all you can *BEFORE* you start to deal.

Optional
Equipment

ONCE YOU HAVE DECIDED YOU KNOW what car you want, you will then need to *pre-determine* how it will be equipped. The optional equipment—*options*—can add considerably to the base price of the car. There are individual options that can cost well in excess of $1,000, and if you choose a variety of the expensive options, it is not uncommon to add 50 to 75 percent to the price of an inexpensive subcompact or compact model. (A common advertising practice that's nothing more than a come-on occurs when a dealer advertises a seemingly low price in the newspaper for a particular model, and the customer goes in to find that the only thing available at this price is a completely stripped-down base car. Just about everything else in this model will be equipped with common, expensive options that drive the price up considerably. As you will later learn, this is but one of the seemingly endless ploys in the bag of deceptive practices that's part of the car dealer's repertoire.)

With so many different makes and models available, you may be faced with various option possibilities. These can range from what would generally comprise a "standard" option list to the new and uncommon—even exotic equipment offerings (variable induction control, active suspension, etc.). Because these options will not appeal significantly to the majority of buyers, I will avoid them entirely; I do not think this chapter would serve much purpose if it functioned solely as a glossary. Rather, what the customer must try to do regarding options is to be informed about their price, and to be knowledgeable primarily about their function and their utility. What you want to have is the credibility necessary for an intelligent discussion about them that will lead to intelligent choices. This is a very important component in providing you with the control essential for subsequent successful negotiations.

It is important to note that international car

competition has spawned a lot of amazing technology in recent years. It is imperative that a customer confronted with decisions involving the more esoteric (and expensive) options do some prior research and understand them before starting to deal. There are two main criteria you should question here: (1) is the equipment or engineering cost effective to *your specific driving needs?* and/or (2) is the pleasure derived worth the added cost? Also to be kept in mind when determining whether or not to buy these kinds of options is the fact that it's highly unlikely you will recoup your expenses with any parallel increase in resale value. (Of course, it's always entirely possible that four-wheel steering will be of specific value to the right buyer in a private sale.)

Today it's common for many popular options to be included as part of an option package or "equipment group." These are offered at a discount to what you would pay separately for them, and usually represent a significant cost savings. Unfortunately, they are also often tied to options that cannot be ordered except as part of an option package. For example, power windows, electric outside mirrors, or six-way power seats may all be available as separate options, but if you decide you want to order leather seats, you will find that they only come as part of a "luxury driving package" that also includes the power seats, power windows, and electric mirrors, along with a leather steering wheel. Although this may be an attractive buy when compared to purchasing these items separately, *you essentially have no choice*. Should you happen to be an individual who does not like power windows and would not have wanted them, you're stuck if you decide you want the leather seats. My advice here is to be honest with yourself about what it is that you really want and then compare costs. It's very easy to get caught up in the excitement of the moment and buy things in "groups" that you would not have considered otherwise. Do not forget that the car companies always want to sell more product, and they are savvy marketing professionals who come armed with all the significant consumer data. It is safe to assume that marketing experts have not put these combinations together by accident.

Also do not forget the dictum that *options can mean BIG profits*. This isn't noted to discourage you from buying them, it's just a fact to consider when the salesman starts to hype them. You will probably hear all sorts of blather about safety, comfort, resale value, etc., but all it *really* means to him is more money in his pocket. After all, not everyone "needs" a power remote trunk.

The following are common optional equipment choices. In most cases, these choices should be based on personal preferences and/or cost. They are listed alphabetically along with pertinent advice or points to consider. If required, explanations or technical data are available at the dealership or from the manufacturer.

Air Bag:
- When available, this is often standard equipment. If it is an option, buy it if you can afford it. (The same thing applies to passenger-side air bags.)

Air Conditioner:
- Increases resale value.
- Only consider "factory" air conditioners (as opposed to aftermarket or unit installations).

Anti-Lock Brakes (ABS):
- For safety's sake, they are well worth the money.

Cruise Control:
- Only consider this if highway mileage figures as a factor in your driving.

Engine:
Larger Size
- Important on small cars if highway driving is significant.
- Can be important in performance cars (check horsepower differences).
- Necessary when towing.
- Fuel economy reduced.

Diesel
- It's less powerful and produces smoky exhaust.
- Mileage is increased.
- Easy availability of fuel can present problems.
- Poor resale.

Turbo
- More power with a smaller engine.
- Often poor throttle response.
- Can run hot in constant city driving.

Heavy-Duty Upgrades (battery, cooling system, etc.):
- Usually longer lasting and worth the small additional cost.

Intermittent Windshield Wipers:
- If not standard, well worth the $40 to $50 cost.

Keyless Entry:
- Poor value.

Light Group:
- Good value.

Power Door Locks:
- Recommended if convenience is important.

Power (Adjustable) Seats:
- Not worth the expense unless two different-sized drivers are continuously switching.

Power Windows:
- Recommended if convenience is important. If you have small children, consider an override control.

Rear Window Defroster:
- Worth the expense.

Rear Window Wiper:
- Worth the expense (especially on hatchbacks).

Sun roof:
- Expensive.
- Will increase resale.

Suspension Upgrades:
- Safer and better handling.
- Worth the expense.

BEST DEALS FOR NEW WHEELS

Tilt Wheel:
- Good value unless driving position "fits" perfectly.

Tire Upgrades:
- Safer and better handling.
- Worth the expense.

Transmissions:
Automatic
- Fuel economy decreases.
- Resale value increases.
- Logical for heavy city driving.

Manual
- Fuel economy increases.
- Usually better acceleration.
- Reduces resale value (except for performance cars).

Trim:
- Highest available trim level will give you better resale.

Trip Computer:
- Limited value, prone to break.

Stereo Systems:
- Most factory systems are not up to aftermarket standards.

- The very best factory option systems (Bose, JBL) cost much less than comparable after-market systems, and these *are* a good buy.
- Resale is increased.

Choosing a Dealer

THERE ARE GOOD DEALERS AND THERE are bad dealers. These businesses are simply franchised stores for automobile manufacturers. The dealer has three main functions that will be important to you: (1) he sells the car, (2) he provides service, and (3) he sells parts. Your relationship with the dealer is obviously important to you at the time of purchase. What you also must consider, and incredibly many do not, is that the dealer can be very important for a long time thereafter—check him out!

Today, in addition to the one-brand dealer, the multiple dealership, representing from two up to as many as five or more manufacturers, is becoming quite common. There are a lot of misconceptions about the advantages and disadvantages relative to a dealer's size. I do not think it's wise to set out with *any* preconceptions based on equating price and/or service with size. I've seen small dealers sell at very fair prices due to good management and low overhead, and volume dealerships or "superstores" who sought very high margins because of costly overhead and a "hustle" philosophy. The exact same thing can be said for the service department; its size does not determine whether it will provide poor or superior service. With regard to representing one manufacturer or several—there is no guideline that is constant, and quality will vary from dealer to dealer. Although you may feel that if a dealer only represents Marque X, he will be a specialist and thus you must be better off, this just is not always true. You need to shop around and do a little investigating, for in the end it comes down to management—their business philosophy and their ability to run things right.

You can always walk into a dealership and inform a salesman or the sales manager that you have been considering strongly buying their product, but you have certain concerns and questions regarding dealership operations that you feel must be answered first. You must be prepared to visit more than one dealer (as many as you can) and consider the following:

· **Reputation and recommendations**.
Check the Better Business Bureau and
other agencies to find out about a particular
dealer relative to others. Ask actual customers for candid opinions—they can tell you a
great deal about the service after the sale.

· **Evaluate his sales staff**. Do they appear
to be knowledgeable and can they answer
your questions? Do they treat you in a
courteous and professional manner? Are
they trying to influence you and "high
pressure" you? How about the salesmen's
longevity—is a lot of turnover common or
have several salesmen been there long?
These types of considerations should go a
long way toward helping you determine if
you want to return. And if you choose to,
there's no reason you shouldn't be able to
meet the owner or the general manager.
You may not be able to do it on the spot,
but you can certainly schedule a meeting.
In Part II we'll focus on the salesman with
respect to his methods, and the negotiation process—what you'll need to know and
what you'll need to do.

· **Thoroughly check out the service department**. This is very important! Talk to
the service manager and also the service

23

employees and mechanics if you can. Find out the average time for certain basic services; see if they work by appointment—check and compare rates. You will spend a single day with the salesman, but the service employees are the ones you'll be depending on after you buy. When you visit the service department, observe: does it offer a good work environment? Is it clean, well lit, etc.? If it isn't, then top-flight mechanics will probably not want to work there. In a similar sense, check to find out if the service department has the latest in diagnostic and repair equipment. This would also be a good time to determine what kind of work guarantee is offered, and also to find out what the policy is with respect to loaner cars and a drop-off service.

· **Check out the parts department and body shop**. If the service department is top-notch, then the parts department most probably is also. This may not be true for the body shop, but it is not of the same significance as the other components that make up a dealership. The fact is that the best body and paint people are simply in too short supply to go around. When and if you need body work done, the best thing to do is to start asking everyone you know who runs the best body shops.

· **Location**. Even though it frequently does, this alone should not determine your buying decision. On the other hand, you will service the car regularly, so consider convenience as a very real factor based on your individual needs. For instance, assume that you very much desire a BMW 850 but live in a rural community that's seventy-five miles from the nearest dealer. You're probably not going to want just any local mechanic working on that car's 12-cylinder motor, so you had better consider this prior to buying and be prepared for the servicing problems and inconvenience that are bound to arise. Or, let's assume you're part of a one-car household and will depend on the car as your only way to get to work short of taking a cab or renting a car. Under those circumstances, it actually may be logical to consider purchasing your car from a dealer on a bus line or with a drop-off service. Unfortunately in a case such as this, it may even be wise to reconsider your first choice of car. Sometimes it can be more important to think of location *ahead* of brand.

From another perspective, the dealer's

overhead will often be significantly based on his location. Think about the big, new, fancy dealer with a prime suburban location. This can easily affect how cheaply he can sell cars or service them. If he does a lot of volume, he may indeed choose to take less margin to keep the ball rolling. On the other hand, overhead must be paid, and if his location is A-1, his service top-notch, and his selection excellent, you will probably have to pay for it. There is no hard and fast rule regarding this. You must simply be aware of the options and shop around or you will never know. Sometimes it may really pay to visit an older established dealer in a less-than-high-traffic location, or even one located in a rural setting.

A final possibility and a good idea, if it pertains to what you're considering buying, is to check out a dealership that's brand new. The common worries here would be "he has no reputation, his staff is new and unproven, etc." I do not believe those concerns are really very significant if he represents any of the major manufacturers. If you consider that the manufacturer screened him thoroughly, he's probably well qualified. But he has no repeat customers at this point, no word-of-mouth clientele; new cars are sitting on the lot eating up floor-plan expenses, and there are no customer-used cars yet. This dealer is probably quite anxious to do business. He will most likely go the extra yard to get you to buy from him.

5

When to Buy

TIMING CAN ACTUALLY MEAN A LOT. IF you had a crystal ball that could tell you how the salesman was doing, what kind of a day or month he was having, how much pressure the dealership was putting on the sales manager, and so on, you could work a much tighter deal. There are always times when conditions create a greater sense of urgency or need for the seller. If your negotiation falls within one of these periods, you will most likely have an easier go of it.

The best months to buy a new car are usually January, February, and March, with February probably being the best. This is the time of year when sales are at their lowest, so dealers are anxious to do business. If you're trading, then it's also a good time because the dealer will need to stock up before spring. Another good period is about two weeks before Christmas. No one is really buying cars then and most salesmen are itchy; they're in a slump, and they're also aware that soon they'll have Christmas bills of their own to pay. The only other time you may have any significant edge is during late summer. It's hot, and people are spending on vacations or not buying because of the new models that will be arriving. For these reasons this is another time that the salesmen are sitting on their hands in frustration. This, plus the very fact that new model year cars are indeed coming soon, can make for a particularly advantageous time to consider an overstocked model.

From the standpoint of best time of the month, your chances of writing a good deal will most likely increase as you approach the end of the month. The salesman on a volume bonus has a quota and will be pushing for his "numbers" as the last days are upon him. Also, each additional unit sold over a certain number could mean even additional dollars, so he really has every reason to be more flexible than usual. Sometimes the first three or four days of the month can also be good, and the salesman will write better deals then too. The same logic applies to the beginning of a month—everyone wants to get out of the blocks fast, get some sales, and get those "numbers" early to take the pressure off themselves later; they can then hold for bigger profits the rest of the month because of the cushion this provides.

If you go into a dealer to conduct business in the evening, about two hours before closing, that's also an excellent time for the buyer because you'll be able to create a sense of urgency, yet still have ample time to employ your strategies. The salesman wants to go home; he's tired. If he believes you are serious and are ready to buy—ready to write a check— and sees this as his last chance to make a sale that day, he really cannot afford to play games. Going home at the end of the day with a sale, even at minimum profit, is still much better than leaving having lost one. After all, it's another unit toward his quota and could also figure into a contest or promotion that he's concerned about. Applying similar logic, you should be able to compound your leverage by choosing a Saturday evening. This should be the most effective evening because it's also the last day of the week.

One last timing consideration is rain or snow. Dealerships are bereft of customers when the weather is bad; most people are not prone to walk the lot in the rain. Therefore, the salesmen are likely having a bad day.

So as you can see, timing can indeed be important. A customer who shops for a car only at the time that's most convenient to him or her could be making a costly mistake. If you've previously located the dealer and picked out the specific car you want, you know that it's sitting on the lot when you walk in, and you are ready to buy, then you probably cannot do any better than two hours before closing on the last Saturday of the month (especially if it's been raining all day)!

6

Your Old Car—
Sell or Trade?

THE BASIC RULE IS THIS: TRADING REP-
resents convenience; selling will most likely
bring you a higher price. Having said that,
consider these two important points.

- If you sell your car before you buy, you may
  have created an impatient and urgent attitude toward buying. You could very well
  end up buying a car before you find what
  you really want, and/or you could make
  yourself subject to a poor deal.

- If you buy a new car first and then try
  to sell the old one, it could take longer

than you anticipate. You will lose its obvious cash benefit, and unless you're willing to pay double the cost for two license plates and two insurance policies, it will just be sitting. In this situation you may become impatient and settle for less money.

RULES WHEN SELLING

1. Get the car in good shape.

   - Clean the car.
   - Clean the engine (buy a $5 spray can of degreaser and use the 50¢ jiffy wash).
   - Clean the interior and trunk.
   - Wash upholstery if necessary.
   - Touch up small nicks.

   (Note: these things should also be done if trading—the dealer thinks "wholesale cost" but he always has some flexibility based on condition.)
   You may want to look into having an auto detailing shop prep the car. This usually costs from $75 to $100, and can

be well worth the charge, especially for expensive or luxury cars.

2. Set a realistic time limit—one month is more than adequate.

3. The price must also be realistic if you want to attract buyers, but leave yourself some room to negotiate.

4. Have a good idea what the retail value is. Check to see what similar used cars are selling for in the papers and on car lots. (Another possible source you can use is the *NADA Used Car Price Guide*. It's available at your bank, at libraries, or in bookstores.) It would also be wise to have a realistic idea of the car's wholesale value at this time. You may discover that it's not worth the time and effort to try to sell your car. (The next section explains how to determine the wholesale price.)

5. Always advertise emphasizing the positive features that are applicable. Some examples: perfect condition, low miles, CD/stereo, one owner, always garaged, never smoked in, leather interior, all service records available.

Other tips:

- Run an ad in the newspaper for one week (not just one day).

- Have a "for sale" sign with your phone number in the car's window.

- If you can do without driving your car on the weekend, leave it parked in a high traffic area such as the parking lot of a large shopping center, near the main entrance area.

- Use bulletin boards at work or wherever available.

- Investigate a professional referral service. They can be a good source of customers and the fee is based on selling the car.

- If you have a contingency deal for a new car that's based on selling yours, offer the salesman $50 for a referral sale (usually referred to as a "birddog fee" in the car business). He has *his* sale riding on *your* sale—it may amaze you how much a well-connected salesman can help in this.

- Another possibility is for a dealer to sell your car on consignment. Check this out and determine if it is time- and cost-effective to your needs. This can be particularly useful if you have an expensive or sports car and are able to wait up to two months for the right price, but do not have the personal time or inclination to do the selling yourself. Get everything in writing and retain the right to remove your car at any time.

Once you have a buyer for your car, you will have to furnish him or her with the title and possibly some other papers. Check with your state Bureau of Motor Vehicles for the specifics beforehand; it should all be very simple.

Advice that I emphatically suggest you heed when selling your car is: NEVER accept a personal check. Insist on cash or a certified check or money order.

THE TRADE-IN

As stated already, trading represents convenience—drive in the old, drive out the new! No ads to run, no phone calls, no time used up showing the car to "shoppers," no paperwork, no continuing liability. And with regard to money: one, the trade can be the down payment for your new vehicle, and two, in many states you will save money by only having to pay the sales tax on the difference after your trade has been deducted. For example, assuming an 8 percent sales tax:

> $20,000   New car price
> -$10,000   Trade allowance
> $10,000   Difference x 8% tax = $800

If you sold the same car through an ad for $11,000, which is only $200 more than the post sales tax price, and factored in the time, the trouble, and your costs, I think the conclusion would be obvious. Sell your car privately only if you calculate that you're sure to come out ahead.

If you do decide to trade, then it is imperative that you learn what the car's wholesale value is *before* you go in to deal. This is the amount your car is actually worth to the dealer or a wholesaler. The way to find this out is to go to four different car lots in your city (two independents and two dealers) and get a *firm offer* for the car. Tell the same thing to all four: say you will be selling for the best price you can get, that you will be going to several other places, and that they're the first one you've talked to.

Do not put any value on "blue book" prices. These merely represent average prices that particular models have sold for. Shop your car to determine its true wholesale value. You may find out that trading is well worth it because there's just no real financial benefit to a private sale. (Some of the pitfalls that can beset you when trading with the dealer are discussed in Chapter 9.)

7

The Test Drive

YOU NOW HAVE A GOOD IDEA OF WHAT
you want to buy, or have narrowed down the
choices, and you want to compare. It is at this
time that you should get a feel for what it's like
behind the wheel. What is important to do is to
arrange for your test driving to be done *prior* to
the day you will be buying.

When arranging this with the salesman,
there are two requests you should make: (1)
ask for a demo that is the same model and
engine size that you will be buying, with as
many of the same options and equipment as
possible, and (2) tell the salesman you'll want
to drive other cars to check out any specific options not on the demo. (For example:
it is unlikely you would buy a stereo sys-

tem for your home without listening to it, so why pay $1,200 for a car system without doing the same? Feel free to bring some of your favorite tapes or CDs and give it a try.)

The following is a test drive checklist of things to do and what to look for.

- Adjust seat, steering wheel (if possible), all mirrors and fasten the seat belt. Do you feel comfortable, and do you have good visibility all around?

- Check all of the controls and options. Make sure you look at *each* one, and if you do not understand what it is or how it operates, ask for it to be fully explained. Are you able to reach comfortably all of the controls? Can you see them all?

- Start the car and let it idle; listen for any sounds that you are curious about.

- Does the car accelerate smoothly, and is there sufficient passing power to suit your driving needs? Make sure you drive it on the highway at speed.

- Is there enough power to climb steep hills if this is a factor in your driving?

- Does the car meet your handling and cornering requirements? Drive it over bumps and rough surfaces and listen for structural integrity.

- Check wind noise at speed. Also check wind noise with regard to open sunroofs, T-tops, and convertibles if applicable.

- With an automatic transmission—does it shift smoothly and at the correct times?

- With a manual transmission—does it engage gears easily, and is the clutch effort not too heavy for your individual needs?

- Are the brakes too light or too heavy (pedal pressure and response)? Do they lock up easily? Make some hard stops if you can.

- Pay attention to engine noise at different speeds and under hard acceleration. After driving, does it idle smoothly at stops? Listen for any noises, rattles, or vibrations that may exist at different speeds or at idle.

- Check the car's dimensions. Is the back seat big enough for your uses? Leg room? Head room? Is the trunk adequate for your needs?

The reason for the test drive is simple, and that is that you will not really know what a particular car is like until you have driven it. And remember, the longer you drive it, the more you will know—a car purchase represents a lot of money, so do not make an expensive mistake in this regard. If necessary, go to several dealers if you feel that you need more time behind the wheel. Be certain you feel satisfied and have no doubts.

One thing you may want to consider is renting the model you're interested in for a day or two. This could cost you up to $100, but if you are not confident or are between models, this could furnish you with the broader experiences that you may need to objectively make a less pressured evaluation or comparison.

Whatever else you do, utilize the test drive for the purpose of *eliminating* any ambivalence or uncertainty about the car itself.

What You
Need to Know
to Get the
Best Possible Deal

The Salesman
and How
"The System" Works

As I explained in the Introduction, a car, unlike most consumer goods purchases, is bargained for. You'll be doing this for a sizeable amount of money, and it is something that you rarely do. On the other hand, the salesman does this every day. This is how he earns his living. He is adept at it, and he assumes you're not—it's right here that you are able to gain a huge advantage. If you know how the system works, if you know what the salesman knows, what he is going to be trying to do before he does it, then it is YOU who're going to have the edge from the start. After all, one powerful advantage you already have over him is the key fact that you can always *just walk away*. If the salesman is not yet at the dealer's lowest price and he believes you're about to walk, then what that represents in his mind's eye is "the opportunity for making $ $ $" walking away. He's not going to give the car away, but rather than earn zero, he most certainly can be bargained down to the price that's fair to you.

THE SALESMAN

By and large, the car salesman depends upon your ignorance. Most are not very professional, and very few are experts about cars. However, what they are very good at, what they are trained to do (their primary function if you will), is to sell at the highest possible profit they can. This maximum profit extends to everything they will sell you, from the car and its options, to any ancillary services and warranties, right on through to the financing if possible. They're not working to be your friend, and they're definitely not a consumer protection society. They are there to part you from your money without you really being aware of what's going on. Even if you find one who's a real "pro"— years in the business, knowledgeable, lots of contacts, numerous "salesman of the month" or "salesman of the year" plaques hanging in his office—all this should do is to make you even *more* wary. A flashing light is alerting you: this guy really knows how to size you up, this guy really knows how to sell cars, this guy really knows how to make money!

Unfortunately, when it comes down to a choice between saving customers money and increasing their own incomes, salesmen are not inclined to be an honest bunch. I'm not implying that they're all crooks, but the system most certainly is not one that is based on candor; to the contrary, the bedrock of their game is founded on deception. You will be told there is no discount when one can surely be had, or quoted the wholesale value of your trade as some bogus "allowance" figure, or convinced of the "value" of rustproofing and fabric protection, or charged a dealer prep fee twice, or told it is only a "one-day sale" price.

The list is endless and my intention is to make you aware of all of this. The bottom line is that if you are not informed, you will pay more, *much more*. You must always remember, no matter how you may feel about him, the salesman is NEVER on your side. Do not rely on him and expect to get a good deal. He will size you up, and then do what is effective to sell the car and make the maximum amount of money possible. So, as I hope you can plainly see, when I say that car salesmen are often loose with the truth, misleading, or just downright dishonest, it's because it's just a plain and simple *fact*.

I am not suggesting salesmen are not smart, or at the very least "street smart." They know you're spending your time in an unfamiliar setting, and that it is their turf. They're aware that in most sectors of society people are inclined to be influenced by and believe the "expert" they've gone to. Whether it's the doctor, the accountant, the electrician, the tennis pro, or the piano teacher, most people rightfully feel they can believe the "experts." After all, this is their job, they're trained, they're experienced, they know what they're talking about, they're truthful—stop right there, because in this business, "it just ain't so!"

Inasmuch as it's common knowledge that some doctors will perform an operation that the patient doesn't need, don't you think it just might be possible that a car salesman will sell you unneeded car undercoating? Along with the fact that the salesman will lie or mislead you, he has many other means at his disposal in such a perfect setting. He will make you comfortable, be friendly and responsive, but you need to realize that this is nothing more than a game of "trust me." Do not confuse niceness with getting a fair price, and always remember that if you trust the salesman, it will cost you.

Intimidation is another useful tool. Again, this works because the buyer is uninformed; thus the buyer feels unsure. The anxiety this creates is perfect for the salesman. He'll more easily be able to bluff and exaggerate, maybe even bully—in short, he becomes the authority figure in the transaction. (Those who are particularly vulnerable to this tactic are older single women, first-time buyers, and lower economic groups or individuals unsure about their credit or ability to finance.)

A successful salesman has developed countless other methods. He will manipulate you by appealing to your ego and playing to psychological weaknesses: "you are what you drive" or "today *everyone* buys paint protection; it's only smart." If it seems appropriate, he will try to confuse you or wear you out; you've been there too long, you're tired, you've tried your best to wade through so much malarkey, that you'll sign a deal just to escape the hassle and get finished. He'll play a discount "shell game" with you, he'll "lowball" you, or he'll "T.O." you (turn you over to someone else); the list goes on and on! But once again what it all comes down to in the end is the simple fact that for the salesman to succeed, regardless of his skill or his ploys, you must be ignorant or uncertain about the car buy-ing process. When you are finished with this book you should not be vulnerable, because you will know how the business operates. Then it just becomes a game for *you* to win.

HOW THE SALESMAN IS PAID

All dealers have a set price they must get for a car, and it is not the sticker or "list" price that's on the car. All that is is a manufactur-er's suggested retail price (MSRP). The way you should determine the price you'll want to pay will be explained later, but what you end up paying directly affects what the salesman will be paid. I think this is important to know, for it should serve as a valuable insight to you when you start dealing. There are three basic ways a dealer pays the salesman: (1) he can be paid a percentage (commission) of the gross profit on each sale, (2) he can be paid a fixed amount that's based on a unit-sold plan, or (3) he can be paid by some combination of both. When the salesman earns a percentage of the profit, then you must understand that every dollar you are able to bargain him down is reducing his com-mission. In turn, he will attempt to squeeze every dollar out of the negotiation that he can.

If the salesman gets 25 percent, for example, then every $100 increment means $25 to him personally.

A salesman paid for each unit sold will get a predetermined amount for each car that he sells. This system also sometimes incorporates fixed bonuses based on tiers or levels of total unit production per month. For example: a fixed bonus is set at ten units, at fifteen units, and at twenty units. This method of compensation is not too common and is usually only found in use at dealerships selling relatively high-priced luxury or sports cars having solid demand equal to or even greater than supply. (After all, some cars actually *do* sell for sums *over* the list price, and in this joyful situation the dealer wants to earn the really big bucks—not pay the salesman.) The combination pay plan employs various creative methods, usually some coupling of fixed percentage with amount-per-unit.

This book will later deal with negotiating the final price, and it is written with the assumption of the most likely scenario, which is that you will be dealing with a salesman paid some form of commission. Usually it is a *straight commission* between 15 percent and 30 percent of the "gross profit" (or profit margin) on each car he sells. With the majority of sales, this profit margin ranges from $200 to $2,000. If, for example, the salesman has a sale with a profit margin of $800, and he is paid a 25 percent commission, he will earn $200. In addition, the salesman earns a bonus paid on certain quota figures and is most probably also paid variable amounts that are based on performance incentives, contests, and the like. On top of this, he receives either a fixed amount or percentage of the "aftersell" he convinces you to purchase, and will be paid a certain amount if he leads you to use the dealer's financing. As you can imagine, you represent a lot of money for the salesman.

Later we will examine the various ways you are "sold." For now, suffice it to say that in the final picture, the salesman is ALWAYS aware that his salary, what he takes home each week for a paycheck, *his very livelihood*, is directly dependent on how much he can get you to spend.

Do not let yourself forget that this is nothing like buying a toaster, because in this type of transaction the salesman has a very keen interest in the final price, a *vested* interest in each and every dollar you spend. So this sale will certainly *not be limited* to just the car itself. I do not think I can overemphasize this, because the salesman can be so good, so adroit at gaining your confidence and convincing you he's there to help you out that he will convince you that his suggestions are for *your* well-being, convenience, comfort, and protection. At the same time, the buyer so often does want to trust and feel comfortable, to avoid hassles and confrontations; he or she wants to accept the salesman's advice and his help. Well, Mother Teresa goes to work each day to help people, *not* the car salesman. Maybe a coach wants to give you good advice, perhaps your father cares about the importance of truth, and your good friends care about being a friend. The salesman . . . *HE goes to work to sell cars for as much money as he possibly can—YOUR money.* At this point even cautious, suspecting buyers are taken in because they choose to be trusting in some way. When you start to deal with the salesman, always keep in the back of your mind the fact that you are his paycheck; you are nothing more than another buyer who walked into the showroom, and the final amount of your total purchase represents the final amount of his income.

THE SYSTEM

All salesmen are trained to use a system when selling a car. This can vary somewhat at different dealers and may be based on the experience of a particular salesman, but essentially he is trying to move you up a step-by-step method that keeps him in control of you. The salesman will be friendly, he'll be polite, he'll attempt to gain your confidence any way he can. (Gaining confidence is what a con man does best, and a car salesman is basically one variety of con man.)

The salesman will "size you up" and decide the best way to go about finding out as much information about you that will help him in his sale. He'll probably start by asking direct and indirect questions that will feed him useful data regarding your job (income), marital status, children, where you live, a trade, financing, etc. After looking at the car with you, he'll discuss it and your needs, emphasizing positive points where pertinent or trying to "move you up" to a more expensive model if he thinks he can make it logical or attractive for you to consider. This will be followed by the test drive. It is usually after a favorable test drive that he'll try to get the sale, and he'll want to know if you're ready to buy the car. He will get you in the office and try to write it up, countering any concerns or misgivings you may have, and it's at this point that negotiation usually begins. Eventually he will write a purchase commitment on your part, padding it with unnecessary extras and/or false charges if you let him. Next, he'll take it to the sales manager for approval or for a counteroffer. This can occur several times if you negotiate strongly. If you still do not reach an agreement together, then the last step would be to T.O. you. This is when the salesman "turns you over" to a manager or some other individual who is a strong closer in order to obtain the price he wants or possibly to "bump you up" before finalizing the transaction. Although you have now reached a deal regarding the car's price, you still cannot relax, because you're not home free, not by the proverbial long shot. Now begins the "aftersell," a process where a dealer takes his last shot at reaping the BIG profits. He will attempt to sell you what essentially amounts to unneeded services, warranties, service contracts, insurance, etc., and hopefully an inflated financing deal.

The entire system is designed to intimidate the customer and to place the salesman in control, to make the customer believe that the dealer is actually doing something for him or her. He's doing you a "favor" by letting you buy this particular car at such a good price, and then he'll take care of you further by looking out for your other needs, seeing to it that you're sold all the other services you could ever need. What a pal! Of course, the major portion of this entire process is just so much baloney. It is based at best on misinformation, deception, double-talk, and gross sins of omission; at worst, on bold-faced lies.

In the next chapter we'll go through the

myriad methods and deceptive devices used as the salesman tries to make his sale. We'll examine the phoney come-on and hype, and you'll be made aware of how to decipher whether what you're hearing is fact or fiction, and how a deceptive statement should be countered or ignored. You will also be able to identify the deceitful ploys utilized as the salesman attempts to sell you something you will either not need at all, or can buy for a great deal less. Once again, you shall see that information is power. If you are able to distinguish what is truthful and what isn't, then you can't be exploited.

9

What You *Must* Know *Before* You Go to Buy

BE PREPARED—DO YOUR HOMEWORK

It cannot be overemphasized how important it is to understand that being well prepared is the primary essential, the single most significant factor when you venture into "the land of the car salesmen." Even if you get less than a "star" salesman, the simple truth is that *he will be prepared,* if for no other reason than that he does this every day, has you on his turf, and has a solid working knowledge of the basics. If you do happen to get a "star," a real pro, then if you're not prepared, you might as well just hand him a signed check. In addition to having mastered all the basics, this guy also understands people, understands sales psychology, knows how to adapt himself to the various reasons for buying, and says what you want to hear. He'll always have logical-sounding answers or glib counters ready. He's able to alter his verbal skills and will be well suited to selling a variety of customers from differing walks of life. He has the necessary patience, and in addition to these and other formidable sales skills, he is a straight-faced bluffer and could probably fool a polygraph. Need I say more? In short, you *must* do your homework and be well prepared if you intend to fulfill your objective: to get the best possible deal and save money.

HOW TO DETERMINE YOUR TARGET PRICE

Although you will learn many different ways the dealer is able to increase his profits at your expense, the first order of business is knowing the right price for the car. The most frequently asked question that I hear from concerned or worried buyers is "How can I determine what I should pay for the car?"

The price of a car is an easily confusing topic

because that's the way the dealer prefers it, and I could easily be as confusing by sifting through all of it, but that would serve no real purpose for most customers. As far as the public is concerned, there's a lot of dealer-inspired voodoo economics when it comes to price. The majority of salesmen do not understand it all either. Believe me, there's a lot of math involved here, and only a few people at any dealership know how to arrive at the net profit price. There are factory rollbacks, incentive rebates, and advertising kickbacks, seasonal manufacturer's specials, floor-plan charges that vary, pro rata advertising fees, transportation charges, etc. . . . Can you accurately learn all of these amounts as they would apply? No. If you could, would you even want to try to master the economics of a dealership through reading a book? Furthermore, do you need to? Again, no.

What you are required to know with respect to the car's price is directly related to being able to negotiate with the salesman—you must predetermine what your "target price" is. To do that, you must be able to figure out an amount that accurately reflects all the above-mentioned dynamics of a dealer's profit and comes relatively close to his minimum profit price.

There are three "prices" you should fully understand before you start to negotiate. These are:

The Sticker Price

This is the manufacturer's suggested retail price (MSRP). It will be the same at any dealer, in any state, because this is mandated by federal law. On the sticker will be listed the car's base price along with all factory options and their prices. Do not think of the sticker price as what you should pay for the car regardless of what the salesman may try to tell you. Rather, it is useful for comparison purposes between differently equipped cars or different models. It is also helpful when you are preshopping various dealers' selections, because the sticker price is needed for a "quick method" of determining the *target price,* that is, the price you will set as your "target" to pay when you go shopping. (In addition to the prices that are listed on the sticker, you should be aware that it contains additional information such as EPA/MPG listing, place of origin, statistical information, etc.)

The Base Invoice Price

This is the amount that the dealer paid (not deleted from this amount is a credit or "manufacturer's rollback" the dealer has received that usually runs from 3 to 5 percent). You can find these dealer costs for all American and foreign cars and trucks listed in books published under the name, *Edmund's New Car Prices*.

The Dealer's Minimum Profit Price

This price represents the minimum amount the dealer will sell the car for. It is usually the base invoice price plus freight charges, pro rata advertising charges (the percentage billed to the dealer for advertising), and floor-plan charges (most of the new cars at the dealership are not owned, but are financed, and these charges are the interest costs). To these are added a minimum profit amount of approximately $100 to $200. Remember, the dealer's true gross profit will also take into account his manufacturer's rollbacks and rebates.

Two Ways to Figure Your Target Price

1. Obtain a copy of *Edmund's New Car Prices*. It is available in either an American or foreign car edition (editions for trucks and vans are also available), and

be certain you have the current copy since they are revised regularly during a year. These are available at your local bookseller, newsstand, and library.

Edmund's will provide you with the dealer's cost prices for all makes and models along with corresponding prices for the available factory options. These prices will be listed alongside the sticker prices.

Match the sticker information of the car you want to buy to the cost prices in *Edmund's* and add these up. To this figure add a "buyer's markup" amount of $700, and this total will be your target price. It should be kept in mind that this $700 buyer's markup represents a calculation based on statistical averages and, therefore, can have a percentage variance when normally applied. These averages include the amounts that the dealer pays for advertising, freight, floor-plan charges, etc., and also take into account his percentage rebate or "holdback," which will vary car to car, and can be further affected by differing quota-based incentive plans or the like.

Lastly, a "pack" amount that the dealer may add in is factored into the average minimum profit figure. The average minimum profit will also differ from dealer to dealer, based on variables such as overhead, time of year, and the turn on a particular model. I point all of this out because it would be a mistake to believe that that $700 is a magical sum. It is obviously not a constant amount and, therefore, should not be carved in stone, due to the aforementioned margins for error. Rather, it is to be utilized to provide you with a useable answer to "What should I pay for the car?" If used in conjunction with the second method of calculating your target price, it will furnish you with a very reliable figure. This, in turn, will enable you to successfully negotiate with confidence because ultimately you will be able to pay a price that you know is realistic and fair.

Example:

Base car—dealer's cost	$ 8,250
Options—dealer's cost	$ 2,550
Factory invoice price	$10,800
Add buyer's markup	$ 700
Target price	$11,500

2. An alternative way to determine the target price is easier, but often less accurate than when you start with the currently published invoice prices. This method is particularly helpful in the

event that you want to calculate a price on the spot. For example, it is an excellent way to establish a target price if you're on the lot shopping dealers and looking at various different cars. Simply do this: using the total sticker price that's on the car, subtract the applicable percentages listed below, then add $700 to that amount. This method will also provide you with a target price, a figure with which you should feel comfortable because it will be reasonably close to the dealer's minimum profit price.

Subcompact . . .	subtract 10%
Compact . . .	subtract 12%
Mid-size . . .	subtract 16%
Full-size . . .	subtract 18%
Luxury and specialty	subtract 20%

Example:

Factory sticker	$18,800
Subtract 16% (mid-size)	$ 3,008
	$15,792
Add buyer's markup	$ 700
Target price	$16,492

Note: if the car you are buying is from the previous model year, you'll need to adjust your target price down by subtracting an additional 5 percent off the sticker price. This is a common manufacturer's rebate to the dealer, and so you should be aware of it.

You are not always going to be able to pay your target price. Realistically, there are the mitigating factors of supply and demand that will influence the dealership with regard to selling at the lowest or the highest price. The economy, the time of the year, what particular models the salesman needs to turn, his dealer's statement, these can all affect price. But unless you already know of a specific reason that would create a firm retail price (e.g. you, along with a hundred other people are on the waiting list for the first thirty-five Mazda Miatas that will be arriving next month), by simply doing some research and checking with several dealers regionally, you should easily be able to determine if the car you're seeking to buy falls into such a category.

WHAT ELSE SHOULD I BUY?

The first step to a successful deal has been accomplished: you know what you will pay for the car. After all, that is nothing more than merely knowing how to determine the correct price. The second step involves learning what else you should buy or should not buy and understanding what the correct or reasonable prices are.

Most of the additional services and equipment that follow the car sale exist primarily for the benefit of the dealer. They range from a variety of overpriced services of dubious worth, to flimflams with no value whatsoever. What's so shocking is the fact that although these scams can cost people thousands, they are for goods and services that are either not needed at all, or can be bought at a mere fraction of what the dealer will charge! So, even if you manage to get a good price on a car, bear in mind that there are still countless ways the dealer can cheat you and reap monumental profits. In actuality, for some dealers who sell lower-priced models with narrow margins, the opportunity for big profits is just beginning.

The Aftersell

The profits that the dealer can generate after the sale or trade of the automobile itself can be astronomical (some might say criminal).

Most of these sources of extra income to both the dealer and the salesman are part of the "aftersell"—what you buy *after* you've OK'd the buyer's order.

For some of these, you seem to have little choice, due to a very clever invention called the "second sticker" that is put on the car next to the manufacturer's sticker and lists these dealer charges. Whenever the second sticker began as a concept, its genesis must have sent thrills of excitement up the collective spines of dealers and salesmen nationwide. This was indeed a great creation because these add-ons (such as rustproofing, undercoating, paint sealers, fabric protection, striping, tinting, etc.) have very low dealer costs—but are very, very high profit margin items and services. And the real brainstorm—because it's already on the car, it's a fait accompli: you *must* buy it! WRONG. I suggest completely ignoring the second sticker when negotiating. After you've reached your price, tell the salesman that with regard to the second sticker, you do not want any of it. He can remove it from the car, or he can eliminate the charge, or he can find you another car without it. Or, if you don't mind having these things, offer him 10 percent to 20 percent of their price, which will generously cover the dealer's material costs in the first place. You should never, ever feel obligated to pay for any of it—you went in to buy a car, not fabric protection.

Common Examples of the Aftersell

- **Rustproofing**. This is probably the favorite of the aftersell swindles sold to the unsuspecting buyer. All modern cars are rustproofed at the factory and have warranty coverage for this. Unless you know you're going to keep the car over five years and do a lot of winter driving, you shouldn't even consider it. This literally costs the dealer $20 to $30 and costs you around $200. In addition, the guarantee is usually full of holes relative to regular service inspections, clauses, deductibles, "where did the rust start" disallowances, and other such disclaimers. It's nothing more than a pure profit marketing phenomenon. But if you feel you cannot sleep at night without it, then go to one of the independent, aftermarket rustproofers. You can shop for the lowest price available, and he will at least do a much better job.

  Rustproofing is usually a straight bonus deal with the salesman, and he will earn from $25 to $75 for each job sold. I think it is fairly obvious what will be said by a

salesman talking about the relative merits
of purchasing rustproofing. Once again, the
system is so tainted that it breeds unethical
and biased partiality.

· **Undercoating.** Ditto above.

· **Paint Sealer or Glaze**. This is a new car,
so why would anyone need to put something on the paint? You can buy the same
glaze for approximately $10 a bottle and
apply it yourself, but a good waxing every
four or five months would serve you much
better. The dealer buys this stuff in five-
gallon cans, which works out to less than
$5 per car, so this adds up to well over a
one thousand percent markup! The dealer
surely must be drooling like a tiger that's
in a cage with a lamb.

· **Fabric Protection.** Price gouging at its
finest! You can go buy a can of Scotch-gard,
apply it yourself, and you will assuredly
do a more thorough job. Often, the dealer
does not even bother to apply anything—
just charges for it. All modern upholstery
arrives stain resistant from the manufacturer, so how would you know the difference? There are so many outstanding rip-
offs at your friendly car dealer, but if you
factor in unmitigated gall, equate the neg-

ligible cost to the rapacious markup, and then consider its utter worthlessness, this may well be the greed winner.

· **Pin Striping.** Just consider: $3 worth of material, $15 worth of labor. Do you really want to pay $100 plus? Get this done aftermarket—you'll save at least 50 percent (or know the aftermarket price beforehand and demand the same).

· **Window Tinting.** Again, same story. Shop the aftermarket.

· **Other Dealer-Installed Options.** My advice is simply "Buyer beware." Whatever the option, if you feel you must have it, check the aftermarket first. An independent contractor will usually charge less and do better work, and offer better quality and more choices (stereos and wheels being obvious examples). It's also worth keeping in mind that in addition to probably being a rip-off, the dealer-installed options are not covered by factory warranties.

· **Extended Warranties.** Do not be allayed into the false sense of security that is the foundation of this scheme. This is essentially a service plan that is an add-on to the car's existing warranty, and it preys upon your fear of *large repair bills*. What you should fear here is throwing away another $300 to $500. These warranties generally only cover the engine and critical drive train components, and here you should presume that anything that will go wrong will happen within the regular warranty term. The surface equipment (alternator, brake cylinder, etc.) you would have to pay for anyway; so the odds are squarely with the dealer. Why do you think he's selling this anyway?

· **Credit Life Insurance.** This pays off the car if you die. Right off, if you have no family, why worry about it at all? And if you are concerned about family debt in case you die, then buy insurance from a respectable agent—not the car dealer! Buy the appropriate term policy, and you will pay a much lower premium and get superior coverage. The same can be said for *any* insurance the dealership may offer. My advice is that you begin buying health or disability insurance from a car dealer when you decide to stop going to your doctor or dentist and start going to the car dealer for your medical needs. In any event, you should mentally feel much healthier just knowing you didn't give hundreds of dollars of undeserved profit to the car dealer.

A Final Note

Lest anyone still think that there exists somewhere a scrupulous car dealer, one who stands apart, one for whom principles, veracity, and business ethics are more important than greed, one who believes that making money is secondary to dealing fairly and honestly with the customer—should you be aware of such a Camelot dealership, then most assuredly it would never employ either of the following examples, which are two of the *most common* dealer swindles, and thus so illustrative of the breed:

1. **Dealer Prep and Transportation Charges**. Do not allow the salesman to add a charge for dealer prep or transportation charges to your sales order. These charges were already included in the sticker price, and thus would represent a *double charge*. Just flatly refuse to pay it. This could cost you anywhere from $200 to $400 and is nothing more than a flagrant attempt to steal your money. How many businesses do you know of that "routinely" double charge a customer?

2. **Handling Charges**. These "closing costs" or "processing fees" are nothing more

than the dealer arrogantly assuming you should give him another $25 to $150 for *absolutely nothing!* In fact, many dealerships are so brashly presumptuous regarding this that they have it preprinted on the sales form so you'll believe it is an official or mandatory fee. There is not one scintilla of truth to this. Do not even consider paying it. It is another example of the mercenary attitude you're up against—yet another version of "take money from the buyer, enrich the dealer" scams that are all too prevalent.

Consider these two common examples of the car dealers' insolence toward the buyer. For example, if a dealer averages 110 car sales a month and is able to collect an "official handling fee and processing surcharge" of $95 per car, and another $285 for the dealer prep and transportation, that would calculate to $501,600 a year of pure profit! Over a half-million dollars "earned" for providing you with absolutely zero! The unadulterated gall of it boggles the mind, but incredibly and unfortunately, it is calmly practiced everywhere in the United States on a daily basis. Unconscionable though it may seem, it is nothing more than standard operating procedure and a common method of conducting business in the car sales industry. Can anyone still have any illusions about placing *any* trust in these guys?

Because the dealers were quick to realize the enormous profits that could be generated, the aftersell has become an important and highly successful part of the industry. Even if dealers fail to get much profit from the car or financing, a lot of easy money can be made this way. A customer who's unfortunate enough to fall prey to all of these back-end flimflams could easily be out up to $3,000.

Something very important which you must also remember is that you should *never* announce to the salesman at the beginning your intentions regarding the aftersell! Do not, for example, say you will not be buying these add-ons or paying these bogus charges. Do not say anything at all vis-a-vis the aftersell until you've completed your negotiation and signed a management approved deal for the car. The salesman probably assumes he'll hook you on this stuff, so it's not to your advantage to pop his bubble early on.

For instance, if you were to say to him right at the start that you know the $100 processing fee is baloney and you have no intention of paying it, he'll simply use this fact in his negotiation as a concession to you, while at the same time figuring it back into his margin elsewhere. Worse, he could suspect you're more savvy than average about the basic worthlessness of the aftersell, in which case he'll prepare for the effect this will have on his commission by more firmly holding back on his gross profit.

It's *never* wise to be a know-it-all too early. Some will say it's best to just walk into the dealership with a no-nonsense attitude and your final price—a take-it-or-leave-it approach. Believe me, putting people against a wall is more often than not counterproductive. The majority of the time, to get optimum results, you should play the game. Polite and humble works best at first. It gives the salesman the illusion that he's in control, which in turn gives *you* the edge.

IF YOU'RE TRADING

Although you may have definitely decided that to trade is in your best interest, it would be advantageous *not* to tell the salesman right away. Say to him that you think you want to sell it yourself because you feel this will enable you to get more than wholesale would bring. (Putting it this way allows you to renege later, and also sends him a signal that you understand wholesale, which could be helpful later.) Go ahead and make the best deal you can without a trade. Once you've hammered out a firm price and concluded your negotiation, *then* you can say you've changed your mind and decided it would be much more convenient and

should facilitate financial considerations great-
ly if you traded. Remember, you have followed
the instructions in Chapter 6, so you know
beforehand the actual wholesale value of your
car. You know what it will bring elsewhere, so
there is no reason to accept less. The salesman
will not lose a "done deal" if the wholesale price
is a fair one, because he intends to make a
profit reselling your trade anyway.

The first thing the salesman will do before
getting a car appraised is to try to set you up by
pointing out some negative aspect(s) regarding
your car. This can take many forms: he can
silently walk around it and look at or touch
obvious defects such as dings or scratches, or
he can point out specific things as he tells you
that it will cost quite a bit of money to prepare your car for resale. He may talk about
your model's lack of resale popularity, its high
mileage, *anything* to soften you up relative to
its value. Don't believe any of it, because it's
just a lot of malarkey that can only work if
you have no firm idea of what the trade value
really is.

After the salesman returns with the appraisal, he most likely will quote you a price that's
lower than the one he just received. There
are two things he knows from experience: (1)
many people think the appraisal price is final,
so they don't negotiate that part of the deal,
in which case the margin he's created by this

little hustle is extra money in his pocket or a hedge against some other concession he can later make, (2) even if you do object to the price, it can be turned into an obvious plus for the salesman; he can then say "you're right and I agree with you, let me go see if I can get the used car manager to go higher for *us*." Either way, you've been had. However, all of this should be of little consequence to you because knowing the car's wholesale value spoils his act. You have an alternative place to sell your car and at this point you needn't be coy about it either. Feel free to name the dealer or car lot that will take your car, and depending on how you evaluate the deal going, you may even want to pad the amount by 5 percent.

One word of caution, however: when the salesman says he's going to get the car appraised, it's a good idea to stay with your car. Quite often you will be told that the used car manager or service manager wants to "run your car around the block" and then into the service department for a quick check while you are shopping. I believe it's a mistake to hand over your keys and let someone drive it away. It is not unheard of for an unscrupulous dealer or used car manager to tamper with your car in some way that could make you anxious to accept a lower price.

PLOYS

By now you realize that the salesmen and dealership can be a crafty and nefarious lot, so it should come as no surprise to you that they will employ a wide variety of dubious methods to sell you. Some of these ploys will be used to reel you in, others to get you interested or to "sell" you. Counting on the law of averages, their presumption is that at the very least, one of these ploys should work. These will range from the common to the creative; therefore, it's not possible to provide any type of all-inclusive list—suffice it to say that "Let the buyer beware" should become your favorite epigram when you walk into a car dealership. Regardless of the way something may appear, you should always be cognizant of the fact that anything said, and everything done, has but one purpose for the dealer—to get you to buy a car as closely as possible to his terms. Here are some oft-used ploys of which to be aware:

24-Hour Sale/Tax Sale/Tent Sale/Etc.

ANY sale is a load of garbage. Sorry, customer, but the car dealer does not operate like

Saks. There are no markdowns. So, unless you like balloons and flags, forget waiting for a sale, because it's nothing but nonsense. Never, ever, will a dealer sell you at one price today, but refuse to do so tomorrow. This is a bottom-line business; the price does not change because it's Washington's birthday or because they're staying open until midnight! The same price is always available. The only valid exception, where there may indeed be a legitimate time constraint, is with a manufacturer-sponsored rebate or financing deal.

Free Air Conditioning, Free Rustproofing, Etc.

PLEASE! Give yourself a break! As is the case above, this is pure bunk. There's no free lunch, no free anything. It all just comes out of the profit margin. The dealer is still looking at the same minimum profit price. Remember that just as a magician creates an illusion of belief, the car dealer creates a delusion for the customer—the belief that if the customer acts *now,* he or she will benefit in some way. This may be resourceful, it might even be ingenious, but it is always false.

Dealer's Discount Coupons

Worthless. More bogus hype.

Sold Below Cost

Rubbish. Dealers will not do it. Do not trust this place at all.

Lowball

This occurs after you've negotiated and reached the point where either your offer can't get approval or you will not pay what they want. As you're about to leave the showroom, the salesman gives it one last shot. He tells you something to the effect of this: if you make the effort to return tomorrow, then he'll make an effort also; he knows another approach that should get the price down *even lower* than the one you're currently at. Then he'll throw out some attractive figure that will get your attention. Another lie. This is "lowballing" you, a ploy to get you back.

Lowballing accomplishes two things: it leaves you with an unrealistic price that freezes you out of a deal with anyone else, and it gets you to return to the dealer.

Ah! The salesman has lived to fight another day, and when you do return, you'll hear one of one hundred excuses why, try as hard as he did, he couldn't make things happen for you. Then he'll start on you again from some other angle, although you'll really be where he previously left off. It's all part of a proven "wear-you-down" method. You've been thinking about the car all night, you saw yourself in it, you were actually making plans around your new car. It very often works.

Should you be lowballed, tell the salesman you appreciate that kind of effort, and at that price, you have no reason to return tomorrow— you would be delighted to buy then and there. Say that you want to go see the manager *right now* for the OK, and you'll write a check immediately thereafter. If he refuses, press him. Ask him why—what's he trying to pull? I doubt if you will have any success, but maybe, just maybe, you'll end up with a car at an unusually low price.

Switching

Be particularly wary of the salesman who attempts to "move you over" to another car or model. If he sounds too convincing, then the car probably has a higher profit margin or pays a bonus to the salesman for some reason, or he may already have a potential customer for the car you're looking at who he knows will pay a higher price for it. There *is* a reason, and it's doubtful that it is in your best interest. Be logical—you know you're standing in the temple of avarice, you know that what you pay determines what the salesman will earn, and you should know that no salesman would have any other real reason or could care one bit what car you'll be driving the next three years. Dubious, isn't it?

Bait and Switch

This is the same scam that is perpetrated on customers for any number of consumer products. The majority of people who are aware of this illegal ploy probably think of it in terms of a sales technique for suckering someone into buying a more expensive television or refrigerator. But surely you must realize that the car salesman is no less corrupt than the local appliance salesman. The bait is a "particular car" that is advertised at a price that is truly a *very* good deal. Of course when you get there, the salesman feeds you some line about being sold out of that "particular car" and you're shown (switched to) a more expensive model.

The Raise

This occurs after you have negotiated a price, signed the order, and given the salesman your deposit. He leaves you alone awhile (he's most likely doing nothing) and then returns with some version of a tried and tested story about how your offer is much too lopsided in your favor. This is such a *bad* price for the dealer—which of course implies that it's such a *great* price for you—that to make it workable they'll need at least the small additional sum of $——. Even adding this sum, the incredibly low price you're paying will still qualify you as shrewd buyer of the month! This is the raise, and it's another flagrant attempt to get more of your money. The salesman has spent a lot of time sizing you up, so the raise is usually left to his judgment. Lest you still wonder how mercenary a dealer can be, it's a pitiful fact worth knowing that this ploy will more often than not be used on the poor souls who already have a bad deal rather than the buyer who's worked a good one. The theory here is that the customer sitting on a lousy deal has been identified as a fish and will probably be gullible enough to pay still more. Profit is profit, so why show mercy? If the salesman can get another $125 out of the customer, why not try?

If this happens to you, do not mince words, say you signed an order in good faith, ask for your deposit back, and tell them you're leaving. You needn't worry, the salesman will accept the signed deal. He may wait until you're halfway out the door before he decides what to say, but he'll find a way.

TURNOVER

As explained earlier, this occurs when your salesman decides you should be "turned over" to someone else at the dealership, usually the sales manager or some other "manager" whose chief function is to increase the final price or "bump you up" before closing the sale. Isn't it great that you get to meet another employee? Just remember that the only motive for the T.O. is the same nocuous one that is the underlying reason for *all* the salesman's ploys—money, *your* money.

Similar to the raise, the T.O. is a strategy that's not necessarily used just to boost a too small profit. Once again, the pathetic truth is that someone who unfortunately is ready to sign a high-profit deal will be further victimized by a T.O. precisely because he or she has been correctly perceived as an easy mark. Either way, it is more of the same: "Gosh, you heard my manager, he says the deal isn't fair to us and he won't go down.

He's going to refuse it unless we come up at least $125, but I think just maybe he might OK $100. I think I can talk him into accepting $100." Such a farce! But nonetheless, amazingly successful. Just imagine how much extra money this can put into the dealer's coffers each year. Pay no attention to a T.O. whatsoever. It should in no way alter your goals.

FINANCING—THE LAST HURDLE

There are different ways the automobile can be financed, and it's important that you know your options *before* you buy a car. Even if you have the cash to buy it outright, it may not be the cost-effective thing to do. If you have access to low rates, then by all means, investigate what it would cost to borrow against a CD or some other financial instrument you could use the cash for; you very well might be better off.

An inexpensive source of financing for a car is a home equity loan. The rates are usually very good, and 100 percent of the interest is deductible. (Since 1990, this is no longer the case on regular bank and commercial loans.) But know that this is a loan for which your house is used as the collateral—do not take out this kind of loan if you have any relevant financial concerns.

Another source of inexpensive money is borrowing against a life insurance policy; these rates might also be cheaper than using cash or liquidating a good investment. There's absolutely no reason not to be creative about your loan just because it will be used to buy a car. If you're able to employ certain sophisticated ways to borrow, then by all means look into them. However, most people electing to finance a car will use one of three common means: a commercial bank, secondary financing, or dealership financing.

Commercial Banks

Banks typically charge interest for a new car loan that is close to that of a home mortgage and most often will require a down payment of approximately 10 percent. The loan officer will furnish you with all the information you need regarding the monthly payments, rate of interest, finance charge, requirements, and insurance costs, and explain any other specific obligations such as default and repossession. From an ethical standpoint, you're usually safest with a bank, especially providing you ask the right questions. With the exception of credit unions, banks are typically the best way to go for financing.

Secondary Financing

These are sources of money other than banks. If you belong to a credit union, it is generally an excellent place to borrow money for a new car. They usually have rates comparable to, and sometimes better than, the banks, and often require no down payment. But not all credit unions are the same, so investigate the requirements and obligations before you decide.

Loan companies charge anywhere from high interest rates (15 percent) up to absurdly, ridiculously, high interest rates (24 percent). Use a loan company as a last resort, and be certain that you understand the installment contract fully before signing. This written contract, along with an office and a desk, are quite often the only things separating some loan companies from your local loan shark.

Dealership Financing

Getting your loan from the dealer's finance manager is akin to dealing with the salesman, in that once again, you'll be acting very foolishly if you put your trust in him. This "manager" is nothing more than a salesman in that he gets paid a commission on any extra interest he can cheat you out of. Cheat is the operative word too. Can you imagine negotiating with a bank officer interest charges that may slide up and down anywhere from one to ten percentage points? When confronted with the finance manager, what you say is that you will pay 1 percent above the going bank rate or you're walking away from the deal. Unless your credit is very bad, you control the situation, not him. Your leverage is simple and rudimentary: no financing, no car sold. And dealers are in business to sell cars, not financing.

One good deal you *can* take advantage of at the dealer is the manufacturer's offer of a low interest rate. This occurs when G.M. or Chrysler or Mazda—the company who manufactures the car you're buying—is offering a rebate in the form of cheap interest. You will usually have the option of a cash rebate too, and if that's the case, you might be better off with the cash and your own loan deal (the cash could be used for the down payment). Car companies are the marketing pros; they realize that a lot of people who do not have any idea what constitutes a "good deal" on a car are on the other hand aware of the fact that a very low rate of interest is a good deal. Customers will jump at the opportunity to pay 2.5 percent interest, while at the same time more than offsetting this financial gain by paying an inflated price for the car. It's really just one of the oldest dealership financing schemes that's been prepackaged in a different guise. However, if you put aside the fact that a rebate or manufacturer-sponsored low interest is available, and use the information you've learned in this book to negotiate a good deal first, then these two manufacturer's promotions can indeed be very attractive.

My advice is this, look for a simple interest loan and then arrange for your loan *before* you go shopping. There's always some fluctuation on car loans, so no matter what your credit worthiness may be, it pays to look around. Let me underscore this by pointing out that just one percentage point on an average ($12,000) three-year loan will be over $200. The potential savings is well worth the time it takes to make three or four phone calls. If after investigating financing, you discover you cannot borrow at reasonable terms the sum necessary for the car you want, then you would be further well advised to re-evaluate your automobile needs.

After You Go
to the Dealer—
The Negotiation and the Purchase

WHEN YOU WALK INTO THE DOOR OF the dealership, remember that although this will essentially be an adversarial relationship you are about to begin between you and the salesman, you want to try to create a cooperative climate. In addition to other factors, this will facilitate your evaluation of him so you can decide if you trust him "enough" to want to buy from him in the first place. You've done your homework, so you needn't waste time.

Begin by being direct regarding your interest in a specific car or model. This allows you immediately to be perceived as a potential buyer. The salesman has little interest in lookers, but he's very willing to invest the time and do everything he's able to to make a sale.

The way you approach this initial contact is very important for a variety of reasons. It will take some time before you are offered the deal you are seeking, and because the salesman is not used to too many customers who react to his sales pitch as you are about to, he will become more and more frustrated as you proceed in the negotiation. There is no need to create any unnecessary tension early on which could make him stubborn or put a chip on his shoulder. Consider that he's been trained to be friendly and accommodating at the beginning because he knows it's easier to trust a "nice guy"; there's absolutely no reason why you shouldn't gain *his* initial confidence in the very same way. Later, when you've got him over the barrel, it will be that much easier for him to give in to you, and he'll be more readily accommodating.

Most salesmen will want to sell you "today" and will want to know, "When do you want to buy?" At the time that this is asked, say you are ready to buy today *if* you can get the right deal. Try to be as relaxed as possible and always look directly at the salesman when you are talking. Do not look around or become hesitant, and do not allow him to be evasive about your questions or talk around them. A good salesman may test you with some intentional misinformation or double-talk just to see whether or how you react. Be firm, correct him if you know it's BS that you're hearing, and ask him to explain or be specific if you actually do not understand something. Always convey the message that you like things to be perfectly clear. Should you know some negative information about the car or the dealership, this is an excellent time to air your concern and ask. For example: you've heard that the dealership has been in financial difficulty, or that they experience a lot of turnover and have trouble holding onto salesmen, or that the manufacturer has been sued due to faulty fuel tanks, or that a particular car has had a history of maintenance problems. Any such questions will put the salesman on the defensive, because any time he's busy answering and explaining, you have gained the upper hand to some extent. And if he's not too experienced, tough questions will throw him off of his routine.

The exact method a salesman uses to hype the car will vary, but it is not that important to you because you know beforehand what you want and what you are prepared to pay. When the subject of price is eventually broached, it is better to introduce or counter with an amount that is 3 percent to 5 percent below your target price. (For example: assume you have determined a target price of $13,500. If the salesman says you are getting a great deal because he will sell you the car for "just" $16,600, you would respond with something on the order of

"Actually, that is not close to what I consider a good deal. My idea of a price that's a good deal is $12,800.") What you want to do is start the negotiation so that the salesman feels he's able to "bump" you up to some degree.

The negotiation could go quickly or may take a little time, but in any event, don't be flustered, embarrassed, apologize, or justify yourself. Make your offer and, except for being willing to come up to your target price, you will have to remain firm throughout. The salesman will say your price is impossible, he will try different methods to get you to accept his figure—from intimidation to lying to turning you over—but stick with your price and basically keep quiet.

Silence applies the greatest pressure. The salesman realizes that you understand what you want in a car and what you refused to buy; he sees that you are adamant, and once he perceives that you are willing to walk unless you get the proper price, he will deal. It's important to convey this fact to the salesman. If you show him that this is business to you and a fair price is much more important than the car, you've won. All too often the customer cannot hide his excitement or desire for the car, and the salesman plays on this. Remain emotionally detached throughout—the way you act is as important as what you know!

When the purchase price has been mutually

agreed upon and has received signed management approval, double-check *all* figures and be positive that the paperwork is in order. Before you sign the purchase order, check that everything matches exactly what you agreed upon in your discussion, and do not be in a hurry. If a deposit is involved, it is your responsibility to make it as little ($25 to $50) as possible, and you should pay it with a check or charge card. The reason for this is that you want the deposit to be in your control in case you change your mind, and if you give the salesman either cash or the title to your trade-in, then *he* has gained that degree of control.

SOME ADDITIONAL THINGS TO CONSIDER ABOUT THE NEGOTIATION PROCESS

It is not a good idea to take children car shopping; at best they are a distraction, and at worst they can become an ally of the salesman. This thinking also applies to the test drive. You don't need the entire family or friends along. You want to remain relatively impersonal throughout, and this is impossible under such circumstances.

When you go to buy, plan on giving yourself

plenty of time. Your salesman probably will not acquiesce to your price very readily and may go through several rounds of counteroffers, red pencil a lot of numbers, turn you over to management, etc. Just relax, and transmit the fact that time is not critical. Let them know that you can go to another dealer much more easily than they can get another customer who's ready to buy.

If you're trading, you will be required to sign a mileage statement. Do not sign a statement that is not completely filled out. Do not accept that it will be filled out later, because you will be liable if this is falsely done and then discovered.

FACTORY ORDER

Many customers choose to factory order their car because it enables them to get precisely the model, color combination, and options they want. There is nothing wrong with doing this. In fact, some dealers like it because it's a certain sale with no floor-plan or other costs. You will want to negotiate your best deal just as you would for a car that's on the lot, but before doing so, there are certain things about ordering from the factory you should be aware of.

The predominant problem you can encounter in factory ordering is delays. The delay can be for a legitimate reason such as strikes, or you could be the victim of a lowball tactic where the salesman writes up a very good price to take you out of the market, later comes up with phoney stalling delays, tells you the price has gone up in the meantime, and then, preying on your impatience for your new car, informs you that the deal must be reconstructed to reflect this increase. Do not be a victim to this scam, and make sure your purchase order has a clause that states an automatic, time-cancellation date. This will give you the right to cancel and receive a full refund of your deposit if the car is not delivered within a reasonable time period (usually eight weeks or less) for any reason at all.

If you are thinking of trading, you will want to secure a guaranteed trade-in price along with a contingency deal for an amount that deducts this trade-in price should you sell your present car in the interim.

The final thing to consider is that when your factory-ordered car arrives, it is your obligation to accept it. If it is delivered "as ordered" and all the equipment checks out, it's then too late to decide the color isn't what you had anticipated or that there are some other reasons why you've "changed your mind." Should this be the case, you will forfeit your deposit.

11

Taking Delivery

WHEN YOU PICK UP YOUR NEW CAR, you ought to be as certain as possible that everything is the way it should be. You are *entitled* to receive a totally perfect and clean car, and you need not take delivery until you are completely satisfied.

I suggest you pick up the car during daylight hours if you can, because it is much easier to inspect the car then. You should also allow for plenty of time in case you encounter problems. The first thing to do is to check the serial number so you know it's the same car you previously looked at and tested. Next, inspect the vehicle thoroughly and check the fit and finish. Drive the car and check the operation of all the controls, making sure any options that you asked for have been included.

If something is wrong or missing, have it corrected immediately or obtain a written and signed document stating that the dealer will fix the problem at a future time at no charge. Do not accept promises! Having not put it in writing, they can always later say, "The spare tire was in the trunk when you took it home." The approach that will produce the best results is to convey the message early that you will not take delivery until *all* problems have been resolved to your complete satisfaction. You have the right to cancel the sales order for breach of nonperformance, and if the salesman knows you are serious about these expectations, the odds are very good everything will be rectified immediately. If you are excited about picking up your new car, it can be difficult to refuse delivery, especially for a small matter; but be forewarned, once the dealership has your money, it sometimes can be very difficult to get the satisfaction or service that is your due.

At delivery check that the following have been done:

- You have been given two sets of keys with key codes.
- The car has a spare tire and jack with a lug wrench.

- Any option upgrades have been installed (heavy-duty battery, sport shocks, performance tires, etc.).

- You have been given the title or title application.

- You have the vehicle registration (if mandatory).

- *All* warranties have been provided.

- Owner's manual has been provided.

- Service manual has been provided.

Leasing

12

What You Need to Know
About Leasing

LEASING IS A WAY FOR THE CONSUMER
to obtain a car to drive without ever actually
owning it. An automobile lease is a contract
with a leasing company or auto dealer that
allows you to use a vehicle for a stated period of time in exchange for your agreement to
pay a predetermined monthly amount. Your
out-of-pocket costs will always be greater if
you lease than if you buy, but the monthly
lease payments will be lower than the monthly
finance payments would be for the same car.
This is because you do not have a down payment to make, and your monthly payments are
calculated on the portion of the car's worth that
you use. What this means is that you subtract
the estimated value of the car at the end of the

lease from its original value at the beginning of the lease, and it is on this difference that the lease is based. So, whereas financing is always predicated on the entire cost of the car, and leasing on only a percentage of that amount, you can see why the monthly payments are less.

This most certainly does not mean that leasing is superior to financing. There are advantages and there are disadvantages. Once you understand what these are, you will be able to apply these factors to your individual circumstances and determine what is best for you. Do not let the leasing agent lead you to a decision, because by and large, leases are usually easy money for the lessor, so you will not be hearing unbiased or impartial information. Do not trust a leasing agent to work for your benefit any more than you would a car salesman. It's *your* job to know the facts before you decide whether to lease or buy.

TYPES OF LEASES

There are two basic types of leases for the regular customer: open-end leases and closed-end leases. The open-end lease is rarely used for the retail customer because the end-of-lease value of the car is guaranteed by you, but it's the lessor who determines that amount. It is rare when this type of arrangement works out to the customer's benefit. Here's how it is designed. At the time that you originally arrange for a lease, the leasing company estimates the projected value of the car when the lease terminates. Should the car be worth less than the estimate, then the lessee (you) will be obligated to pay the difference in cash (it is often stipulated that this will not exceed the amount of three monthly payments). Should the leasing company determine that the value of the car is higher than the estimate, then you will be paid the difference. You probably should harbor expectations of this latter possibility occurring with about the same frequency as do earthquakes. Unless you enjoy high-odds gambling, it seems unlikely that you would want to risk sharing the responsibility for the car's worth at lease end. Therefore, the contract we shall be dealing with will be the closed-end lease.

The closed-end lease is the type most commonly used by retail customers. As the lessee, you're responsible for the car only until you have completed the monthly payment schedule (provided that the condition of the car and its mileage fall within the limits stipulated at the inception of the lease). At that time you have no further financial obligation and can "walk away" from the lease. If you have an option to purchase the car for the cost of the residual or a preset amount, then that must also be stated as a clause in the contract.

FEATURES OF THE LEASE

As is the case when you finance, the lease payments are spread over the term of a car's depreciation. With a lease, the monthly payments are usually lower, *but* at the end of the lease term, the leasing company or dealership owns the car, not you. That the monthly payments are indeed lower than finance payments for the same period of time creates an illusion for many customers to this effect: "because it's cheaper, it's a good thing to do." The simple reality is that that's not true for everyone; and, furthermore, should it be your intention to eventually *buy* the car, you most probably will pay *more* by leasing. Moreover, should you terminate the lease early, the cost will certainly be much greater than on a financed purchase.

An important and attractive feature of leasing is that there is no down payment to make; however, there are usually other cash requirements such as a security deposit and prepayment of the first month's rent to consider. Another concern when leasing is that excessive mileage and wear and tear on the car will cost you an additional cash outlay at lease end, since you are contractually obligated to compensate the lessor for exceeding the stated limits and provisions.

A common misconception about leasing is that you just pay the monthly rental payment and do not have any other charges—nothing could be more wrong. The auto lease involves licensing, registration, and other costs, all of which will be factored into the payment, and a leased car requires servicing and insurance just as the same car would if you were buying.

ADVANTAGES OF LEASING

There are a variety of reasons why a customer may find it advantageous to lease. One of the obvious benefits is cash flow, because you are essentially "renting" a car, not buying it. Your monthly payments may be up to one-third less for the same car, and this extra cash can be applied to other uses or saved. The lease also does not require a down payment or the need for a trade-in. This total amount of cash can easily be several thousand dollars. If you project this amount invested at a reasonable rate of return over a three-year period, you will have a good idea of what the cash value of leasing may mean to you.

A certain comfort level comes with knowing that at a specified time in the future, you can just walk away from the car. You have no concerns or uncertainty about reselling or haggling over a trade. The resale price is guaranteed in advance, so if the car should depreciate more than anticipated, it is the leasing company that will incur the loss.

Another common rationale is that if you made the same monthly payments as you would have made financing (including the down payment), then you could drive a fancier, more expensive car by leasing. Although that may not be a practical consideration, it is the primary reason why a lot of people drive what they drive.

This consideration is particularly applicable if one wishes to drive an expensive car and get a new one regularly. Here is an example of how this works: say you were to lease a $35,000 luxury car that would be worth $20,000 at the end of the lease term. Your monthly lease payment would be *financing $15,000*—not $35,000—plus the interest, licensing, registration, and other costs to the dealer. So, your monthly payments will be much, much lower than if you were to buy the same car. In other words, you could choose to drive an expensive automobile for what your monthly outlay would be to finance a less costly car. But it must always be remembered that at the end of the lease you will have no equity in the car. A good candidate for driving a more expensive car by leasing would be the person who is applying or is allocated a fixed monthly sum and is then able to write off 100 percent of this amount due to business usage.

There used to be tax advantages to financing a car relative to the deductions you could take, but this is no longer the case. The only way leasing is justified from a tax standpoint is to view it inversely to buying. Because you are no longer allowed the larger deductions for buying, and because you have increased your cash flow by leasing, then this may cause you to consider leasing as the more practical alternative. Remember, it's the *use* of a car, not the manner in which you acquire it, that will determine its tax deductibility. If you use your car 100 percent for business, then you can deduct the full amount of the lease payment and all other expenses. If you use it less than 100 percent, you can deduct only the percentage which is applicable. Check with an accountant to determine your rights if you're not certain about automobile deductions.

A final advantage, which will be negligible to many but is a valid reason for some who lease, occurs when an individual feels that he or she is "too busy" to go car shopping, take test drives, negotiate, etc., with a lease, you can pretty much arrange for the new Jaguar over the phone. Of course, this ease (of entry) also applies to the exit, so at the expiration of the lease you have no concerns about selling or trading either. A word of advice, however. If you've never before leased and are considering doing so, with your primary purpose being conveniently arranging to drive a luxury car, be aware that your established credit rating and your income *must* reflect the choice of such an expensive car. Lenders will not easily approve such a lease-loan, due to the fact that cars are a declining asset, and there is no down payment to offset their risk in case of an early default.

DISADVANTAGES

Disadvantage number one is that your out-of-pocket costs will be more by leasing. The other obvious disadvantage is that because you have been paying only for the use of a car, at the end of the lease term you will have no equity—you do not own the car. At that time, you will have to lease or purchase another vehicle. Once you own a car, you are able to calculate that for every year you choose to drive it beyond the three- to four-year leasing/financing period, you will save the considerable sum that the monthly leasing payments would have represented. Allowing for depreciation, this could still easily be anywhere from $2,000 to $8,000 a year. You must be able to ask yourself honestly if you will or will not want to keep the car you've been driving once the lease ends.

If you decide to terminate a lease early, that decision will probably be very costly. The leasing company will determine the current wholesale value of the car and their lost profits, and you will subsequently be charged an amount based on this. It's entirely different from purchasing a car by financing, because in that situation you can always personally sell the car for the highest amount it will bring, with your only liability being the net payoff. Another potential problem when you're leasing is getting stuck with a lemon. Should the car be undrivable for any extended period of time, whether this is one month or six months, you are still obligated to make the payments unless otherwise specified. Reading the fine print regarding this condition should not be overlooked.

Leasing a car can be an overriding disadvantage if you either drive an above average amount or are not too good about caring for a car. Under the terms of most lease agreements, the lessee will pay a penalty for excessive mileage, and he or she will also be charged for "above average wear and tear." The mileage charge normally accrues after 15,000 miles per year, computed as an average over the lease period. For example, if you were to have a three-year lease, you would pay a penalty for any mileage over a 45,000-mile total. It makes no difference how many miles you put on the car in any one year. Penalties can run as high as 12¢ a mile, so I suggest you make an accurate self-evaluation and be clear both about this and the "wear and tear" stipulations.

HOW TO SHOP FOR A LEASE

Leasing companies have proliferated in recent years, and auto dealerships have also enthusiastically jumped into the fray. Why? Because a lot of money can be made—why else? It most assuredly is not for the benefit of the public. You know that the dealerships have refined the selling of cars down to a system, so you'll not be surprised to learn that the same can be said for leasing. If the car dealers are able to "take the customer for a ride" before he buys that ride, then it's easier for the lessor to do the same because leasing is even more complicated and impenetrable to the average customer. If the car salesman is the "shaman of scams," the leasing agent is able to do it with mirrors.

Just imagine that an average customer ventures into a leasing office simply because he has heard it can be *smart* to lease. Here's what he finds out as he's made aware of the "facts": unlike buying, leasing does not involve financing a car to own but merely financing the depreciation over the lease term. How much it will depreciate is estimated by the leasing company, who, in turn, is guessing its value at the termination date. There are open-ended leases and closed-ended leases, and leases that provide buy-back clauses. There is residual value to consider, and mileage clauses, and "wear and tear" stipulations, and depreciation allowances, and capital cost reduction, etc., etc. By the time the average wide-eyed customer finally nods "yes, I *do* understand everything," the lease price has, in the meantime, been calculated from full markup and the contract is signed. Because people do not understand leasing per se, and because the monthly payment price is comparatively lower, they do not bargain the price down. This has made lessors greedy, so it actually is harder to deal when leasing; but dealing still is possible if you know the facts, know what to look out for, and shop around.

The first and most important rule when leasing is that you MUST shop around. Using the phone, shop a mix of several leasing companies and car dealerships, and be prepared to bargain the price with both. Although leasing companies are usually less flexible and end up not going as low as a car dealer will for the same car, you can only expect to get that lower price from the dealership if you're willing to work the negotiation as hard as you would for a purchase. Car dealers by nature start as high as possible, but, in turn, can usually be brought lower through preparation and effort.

Just as it is imperative when buying to do your homework, it is every bit as important when leasing to do the same. Establish what car you want and know the cost price of it *before* you call or walk in. Once you have this information at hand, this is what you should do: call the various companies you've chosen (the more, the better for you) and say that you're thinking about leasing car model X for thirty-six or forty-eight months and are in the process of shopping for the best deal. Point out that you will want a closed-end lease without any type of insurance, any nonfactory options, or any other services of any sort. Be prepared to tell them where the car you want is located if necessary, the annual mileage you will be driving, and know the MSRP for the car you want. Tell them that when they call you back with the quote, it should be final and inclusive of all taxes and charges, and you'll want to know exactly what these comprise. You'll also need to find out the deposit policy, mileage allowance figure and penalty, and be certain about the excess wear and tear clause. Concluding the discussion, in your own way you'll want to imply that since you've negotiated in good faith, you expect this to be the final price and will not even consider accepting a renegotiated deal of any sort thereafter.

If you want to determine where you'll get the best rate, it will take some initial preparation and work. After that, the more you shop the market, the more certain you can be that you've received the best possible quote.

THE TRADE

At the time you begin doing your preparation prior to leasing, if you happen to own a car that you want to get rid of, make sure you've shopped its market value first (see Chapter 6). After you have completed this, I only have two pieces of advice relative to a trade: (1) sell the car yourself if you possibly can (you will very likely get a lot more money), and (2) be prepared for the fact that leasing companies will only offer you wholesale or less (car dealers may do better, but don't count on it).

Note: once a price is agreed upon with the leasing company, ask to receive a separate check in payment for the trade. Unless you are mathematically adroit and feel very secure about that fact, it is a mistake to negotiate the trade as part of your lease deal with the objective in mind of lowering your monthly payments further. This may well be your intention, but the leasing agent sees it as an opportunity to practice his double-talk as he takes you on a journey down the back roads of allowances, trade discounts, and other rip-offs.

OPTION TO PURCHASE

A customer sometimes wishes to have the option to buy the car he's been leasing, and there are two customary ways this can be done: (1) you can sign a contract that calls for the option to be exercised at a fixed purchase price—this clause presets your purchase price at a fixed sum or projected "residual" value, or (2) you can agree to pay a wholesale price to be determined at the lease termination, based on some formula spelled out in the contract. Opt for the former, but first contemplate it and give some consideration to what you know or can reasonably predict about the preconditions. If you know you are going to keep the mileage low, and likewise know that you keep cars in good condition, then the value of the car will probably be greater than the option price. Or, if you are buying a car that traditionally holds its market value very well, the predicted value could be underestimated as well. In these situations, even if you don't want the car, you can always realize a nice profit by reselling a clean car with a high market value.

The best thing about an option is precisely the fact that it is *your option* to do as you please. You're not compelled to buy anything if you don't want to. It is your choice to make three or four years *after* you sign the lease. If the car isn't worth the option price at that time, or should other financial circumstances rule it out, walk away.

PLOYS

Just as you must beware of hazards and deceptions aplenty when buying, so must you also be careful and well informed when leasing or you will be gleefully taken. As I previously pointed out, the leasing salesman already has the confusion of numbers to shade his ethics. Moreover, the general lack of consumer understanding about the leasing procedure will not serve to lessen his dishonesty and desire for the dollar. By and large, the lease salesman utilizes many of the same ploys that car salesmen use, so you should be aware of them as described in Chapter 9. Quite a few apply verbatim, while others require slight, but obvious, modification on your part to be applicable. Prepare yourself by understanding how the T.O., lowball, and bait-and-switch work, and also be aware of the following ploys as adapted to leasing:

· **Misleading Ads**. Auto leasing lends itself to misleading ads and deceptive come-ons for the very same reason that facilitates so much of its high profit success—lack of customer understanding about how it works. A lot of leasing ads succeed by using figures that appear very reasonable and enticing to the uninitiated. For example: "No money down, drive a new Thunderbird for only $289 a month." Sure, this is possible, but first it is computed based on a sixty-month lease term, and secondly, this quote is for a standard model with no options. On examination, just these two points alone make it clear that it's not such a good deal after all, not one that the majority of customers would want.

There are countless other ad deceptions

that rely on the customers' lack of understanding. These can range from leaving out
the fact that taxes and document fees are
not included in the price, to using terms
such as "equity payment mandatory" or
"cash reduction payment is required"—
both euphemisms for down payment. The
lessor is aware that the average customer does not grasp the business and is an
easy mark; therefore, the deceptions are
only limited by the scruples of the lessor
and the imagination of the copywriter.
My advice is to ignore ads completely.
Do not be suckered by them. Do your
homework, be prepared, and shop around
for deals, rendering the ads as irrelevant.

· **Bait-and-Switch/Price-Jacking**.   Bait-
and-switch will commonly be used in
print ads just as described under car
buying ploys, but this scam takes on additional dimensions in the leasing business
because it is so much better served by leasing's widespread use of the telephone for
conducting business. For example: you're
quoted a price on the phone, but when
you go in you are told some foolishness
about the company not being able to get
the car or approval for the car, and then
you're moved into something else with a
much better profit structure. The telephone

also allows for the unabashed use of numerous ambiguous words and phrases such as "about" or "in the neighborhood of" or "this isn't an exact figure, but around . . ." Do not allow yourself to be jacked-up later when you are in the office because of some false term the lessor tries to slide by you on the phone. Nail him down. Tell him you've never seen a purchase or payment contract written with language like "in the neighborhood of $500." Don't let him jack you up for any reason whatsoever.

Anytime you're talking about monthly payments, remind yourself: multiply, project, figure, extrapolate, fill in the numbers—but do not let it pass because it doesn't sound like that much money. This is what the salesman relies on. Padding the number is probably the A-1 favorite trick perpetrated, because even less than cunning or accomplished salesmen know that $10 a month may not get any resistance if reasonably introduced. But $10 a month for sixty months is $600 worth of pure profit; $50 a month would be $3,000!

THE CONTRACT

You have decided on a lease price that you consider a good deal. Now take the time to make sure you fully understand the lease terms and your liability. Be certain this is clearly spelled out, because once you sign a lease, it is an iron-clad contract. Being careful is only being smart. The government has enacted a law called Regulation M, and this will offer the consumer protection up to a capital cost of $25,000. However, in excess of that, or for a corporate or business lease, you will not be covered.

You should be certain that the following information is contained in the lease contract. Make *sure* you understand everything and are comfortable with the language and description used.

1. Make.

2. Model.

3. Model year.

4. Vehicle identification number (VIN).

5. Purchase option. This should be stated along with its terms and the residual value of the option.

6. Excess wear and tear clause. This should be spelled out in detail, and you

should feel that you understand what these details imply; once you've signed, you've agreed to its definition.

7. Annual mileage figure. This discloses the annual mileage allowed *and* the penalty charges for any mileage in excess of that figure.

8. Early termination disclosure. *Understand* the costs involved and the formula used to determine them.

9. Default clause. This spells out what constitutes a default.

10. Charges and monthly payment schedule. Be aware of the taxes, fees, etc., that you must pay and the lease term.

11. Termination. You should understand what you will be responsible for doing when the lease ends. (For example: returning the car, payment of fees, refund of security deposit, buying the leased car, "rolling over" into another lease, subleasing.)

12. Insurance. The lease will dictate that proof of insurance is required, what level of insurance is necessary, and

will stipulate the payee. You should also consider here any stipulations that may or may not deal with the total loss of the vehicle.

CONCLUSION

It is always prudent to sit down and calculate the cash flow for the lease term as compared to financing the car for the same period. You will have to figure your up-front charges for both financing and leasing, and then your continuing cash requirements. This cannot accurately reflect resale value, potential interest earnings, etc., but it should provide you with relevant cash outlay comparisons for a particular car. Along with cost, it's also important to realistically consider the fact that as a lessee, you will have no equity at the end of the lease. Will you be willing to lease again? Will you want to purchase a car you've been driving (for up to sixty months)? Or, will you maybe want to buy a new car at that time?

By now you should be comfortable with leasing as a concept, and as you've learned, there's a lot that can be said in support of it. Those applications notwithstanding, the main benefit lies in the opportunity the lease provides for someone to pay only for the use of a car, rather than the entire purchase price, without the attendant uncertainty of reselling or trading at the end of the contract.

Appendix

AUTOMOBILE MANUFACTURERS

ALFA ROMEO
Alfa Romeo, Inc.
250 Sylvan Ave.
Englewood Cliffs, NJ 07632

ASTON MARTIN
Aston Martin Lagonda of N.A., Inc.
342 W. Putnam Ave.
Greenwich, CT 06830

AUDI
Volkswagen of America, Inc.
P.O. Box 3951
Troy, MI 48007

BMW
BMW of North America, Inc.
BMW Plaza
Montvale, NJ 07645

APPENDIX

BUICK
Buick Motor Division
General Motors Corp.
902 E. Hamilton Ave.
Flint, MI 48550

CADILLAC
Cadillac Motor Division
General Motors Corp.
2860 Clark St.
Detroit, MI 48232

CHEVROLET
Chevrolet Motor Division
General Motors Corp.
30007 Van Dyke Ave.
Warren, MI 48090

CHRYSLER
Chrysler Corp.
P.O. Box 1919
Detroit, MI 48288

DODGE
Dodge Motor Division
Chrysler Corp.
P.O. Box 1919
Detroit, MI 48288

FERRARI
Ferrari North America
777 Terrace Ave.
Hasbrouck Heights, NJ 07604

128

FORD
Ford Motor Division
Ford Motor Co.
300 Renaissance Center
P.O. Box 43303
Detroit, MI 48243

HONDA
American Honda Motor Co., Inc.
100 W. Alondra Blvd.
Gardena, CA 90247

ISUZU
American Isuzu Motors, Inc.
P.O. Box 2280
City of Industry, CA 91746

JAGUAR
Jaguar Cars, Inc.
600 Willow Tree Road
Leonia, NJ 07605

LAMBORGHINI
Lamborghini of North America
17230 South Avalon Blvd.
Carson, CA 90746

LINCOLN
Lincoln-Mercury Division
Ford Motor Co.
300 Renaissance Center
P.O. Box 43322
Detroit, MI 48243

129

APPENDIX

LOTUS
Lotus Performance Cars, L.P.
530 Walnut Street
Norwood, NJ 07648

MASERATI
Maserati Automobiles, Inc.
1501 Caton Ave.
Baltimore, MD 21227

MAZDA
Mazda Motors of America, Inc.
3040 E. Ana Street
Rancho Dominguez, CA 90221

MERCEDES-BENZ
Mercedes-Benz of North America
One Mercedes Drive
Montvale, NJ 07645

MERCURY
Lincoln-Mercury Division
Ford Motor Co.
300 Renaissance Center
P.O. Box 43322
Detroit, MI 48243

MITSUBISHI
Mitsubishi of North America
West Office Tower
10540 Talbert Ave.
Fountain Valley, CA 92708

MORGAN
Isis Imports, Inc.
P.O. Box 2290
United States Custom House
San Francisco, CA 94126

NISSAN
Nissan Motor Corp. in USA
P.O. Box 191
Gardena, CA 90247

PLYMOUTH
Plymouth Motor Division
Chrysler Corp.
P.O. Box 1919
Detroit, MI 48288

PONTIAC
Pontiac Motor Division
General Motors Corp.
One Pontiac Plaza
Pontiac, MI 48053

PORSCHE
Porsche Cars of North America
200 South Virginia St.
Reno, NV 89501

ROLLS-ROYCE
Rolls-Royce Motors, Inc.
P.O. Box 476
Lyndhurst, NJ 07071

SAAB
Saab-Scandia of America, Inc.
P.O. Box 697
Orange, CA 06477

SUBARU
Subaru of America
7040 Central Highway
Pennsauken, NJ 08109

TOYOTA
Toyota Motor Sales, USA, Inc.
P.O. Box 2991
Torrance, CA 90509

VOLKSWAGEN
Volkswagen of America, Inc.
P.O. Box 3951
Troy, MI 48807

VOLVO
Volvo of America Corp.
One Volvo Drive, Bldg. A
Rockleigh, NJ 07647